Hello, 이솝우화!

개정판

②

Hello, 이솝우화! 2 (개정판)

2007년 6월 19일　초판 1쇄 펴냄
2023년 10월 20일 개정판 1쇄 펴냄

원작 이솝
글 국제어학연구소 영어학부편
감수 이동호
그림 최정현·조한유·유지환
펴낸이 이규인
펴낸곳 국제어학연구소 출판부
출판등록 2010년 1월 18일 제302-2010-000006호
주소 서울특별시 마포구 대흥로4길 49, 1층(용강동 월명빌딩)
Tel (02) 704-0900 **팩시밀리** (02) 703-5117
홈페이지 www.bookcamp.co.kr
e-mail changbook1@hanmail.net

ISBN 979-11-9792043-1 (13740)
정가 16,800원

영어의 기초를 다져 주는

magic

Hello,
이솝우화!

2

개정판

원작 이솝 | 글 국제어학연구소 영어학부
감수 이동호 | 그림 최정현·조한유·유지환

ILR 국제어학연구소

이 책의 특징

　이 책은 아이들에게 친숙한 이솝우화를 영어로 읽으면서, 자연스럽게 영어의 낱말과 표현을 학습하게 하는 책입니다. '이제 막 영어를 배우기 시작한 아이들이 영어문장을 이해할 수 있을까?' 라고 생각할 수도 있을 것입니다. 하지만 이솝우화는 거의 모든 아이들이 이미 알고 있는 이야기입니다. 또한 예쁜 그림으로 설명이 뒷받침되기 때문에, 스토리에 나오는 낱말과 표현을 쉽고도 재미있게 이해할 수 있습니다.

　이 책은 또한 언어의 습득 과정인 듣기 → 말하기 → 읽기 → 쓰기의 순서대로 학습이 진행됩니다. 이렇게 다양한 방법으로 여러 번 낱말과 표현을 익히게 되면, 쉽게 잊어버리지 않으므로 진정한 자기의 실력이 됩니다.

　이 책의 목적은 스토리에 나오는 모든 낱말과 표현을 이해하는 것이 아닙니다. 스토리에 나오는 낱말과 표현 중에서도 중요한 낱말과 표현만을 골라 학습하게 합니다.

　낱말 익히기와 표현 익히기에서 배우게 되는 낱말과 표현만 알아도 상당한 효과를 얻을 수 있습니다. 그러면서도 스토리를 통해서 영어를 익히게 되므로, 기본적인 문장 감각을 몸에 베이게 하는 효과를 볼 수 있습니다.

부모님! 이렇게 지도해 주세요!

1 예비학습

스토리 이후의 학습에서 본격적인 학습이 이루어지므로, 예비학습은 그림을 한 번 보고, 듣는 정도로 가볍게 넘기세요.

2 스토리

스토리의 낱말과 문장을 모두 이해하려고 하지 마세요. 낱말과 표현 익히기에서 배우게 되는 낱말과 표현만 확실히 알게 해주셔도 아주 좋은 효과를 얻을 수 있습니다.

❸ 낱말 익히기와 표현 익히기

스토리에서 나온 낱말과 표현을 익히는 과정입니다. 먼저 MP3를 들으면서 따라 말하고, 따라 씁니다. 이 단계에서는 낱말과 표현을 확실하게 익히는 것이 좋으므로, 필요하다면 MP3를 다시 들으면서 다른 노트에 더 써보는 것도 좋은 방법입니다.

이렇게 확실하게 익힌 후에 문제를 풀게 되는데, 듣기 → 말하기 → 읽기 → 쓰기의 순서로 문제를 풀게 되므로, 보다 쉽고 확실하게 낱말과 표현을 확인할 수 있습니다.

❹ 뽀너스! 뽀너스!

사자(lion)와 쥐(mouse)를 영어로 배우면, 호기심 많은 아이들은 '그럼 다른 동물들은 영어로 뭐라고 할까?' 라는 의문이 생기겠죠? 또 '나는 너무 졸려(I'm too sleepy.)' 라는 표현을 배우면, 그럼 '나는 너무 피곤해.' 는 영어로 뭐라고 할까? 라는 의문도 생길 것입니다.

이 단계는 이러한 궁금점을 해소함과 동시에 같은 범주에 있는 새로운 낱말과 표현을 확장해서 배우게 되는 효과가 있습니다.

❺ Dictation

Dictation은 우리말로 '받아쓰기' 라는 말이에요. 이 교재에서는 단순히 영어 낱말이나 표현을 듣고 받아쓰는 것이 아니라, 앞에서 배웠던 스토리를 그림과 함께 보여주면서, 문장의 빈칸을 채워서 쓰도록 합니다. 따라서 스토리에 대한 이해를 함께 할 수 있습니다.

원어민이 천천히 읽기는 하지만, 한 문장 한 문장을 놓치지 않고 집중해야 빈칸에 알맞은 낱말이나 표현을 쓸 수 있습니다. 만일 놓쳤다해도 MP3를 다시 들으면서 끝까지 모두 쓰도록 하세요.

❻ 스토리 이해하기

이제까지의 학습으로 중요 영어 낱말과 표현, 또한 스토리의 내용을 이해하게 되었을 것입니다. 이 단계는 이제까지 학습한 내용을 문장을 통해서 확인해보는 단계입니다.

앞에서 배운 내용보다는 난이도가 있지만, 이제까지 충실하게 교재를 학습했다면 충분히 풀 수 있는 문제들이므로, 자신감을 가지고 도전하세요!

이 책의 구성

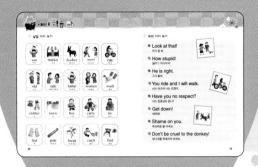

예비학습
스토리를 읽기 전에, 스토리에 나오는
낱말과 표현을 미리 익혀요.

스토리
원어민의 정확한 발음으로 스토리를
들으면서 어떤 내용인지 파악해요.

낱말 익히기와 표현 익히기
원어민의 발음을 그대로 따라 하고, 읽고, 쓰면서
낱말과 표현을 익혀요.

듣기, 말하기, 읽기, 쓰기 문제
앞에서 익힌 낱말과 표현을
듣기 → 말하기 → 읽기 → 쓰기의
순서대로 문제를 풀어요.

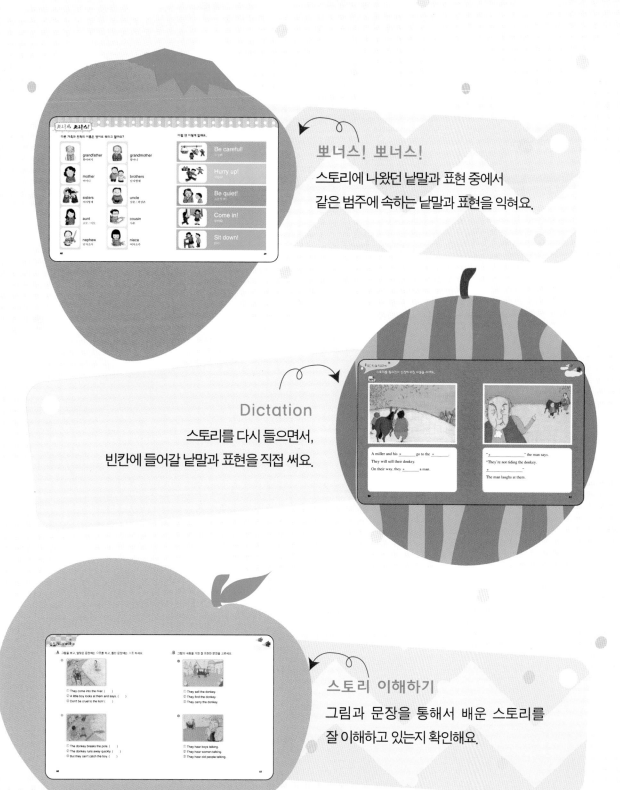

뽀너스! 뽀너스!
스토리에 나왔던 낱말과 표현 중에서
같은 범주에 속하는 낱말과 표현을 익혀요.

Dictation
스토리를 다시 들으면서,
빈칸에 들어갈 낱말과 표현을 직접 써요.

스토리 이해하기
그림과 문장을 통해서 배운 스토리를
잘 이해하고 있는지 확인해요.

차 례

The Miller, His son, and the Donkey · 10

The Ants and the Grasshopper · 64

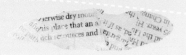

The Honest Woodcutter · 118

우리말 해석과 정답

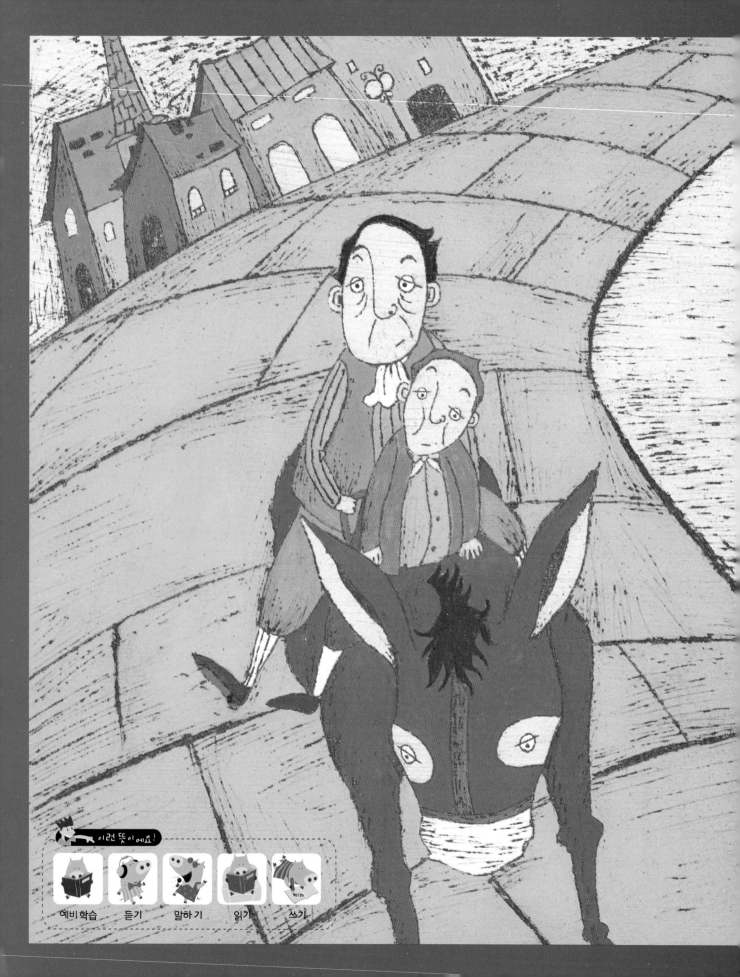

이런 뜻이에요!

예비학습   듣기   말하기   읽기   쓰기

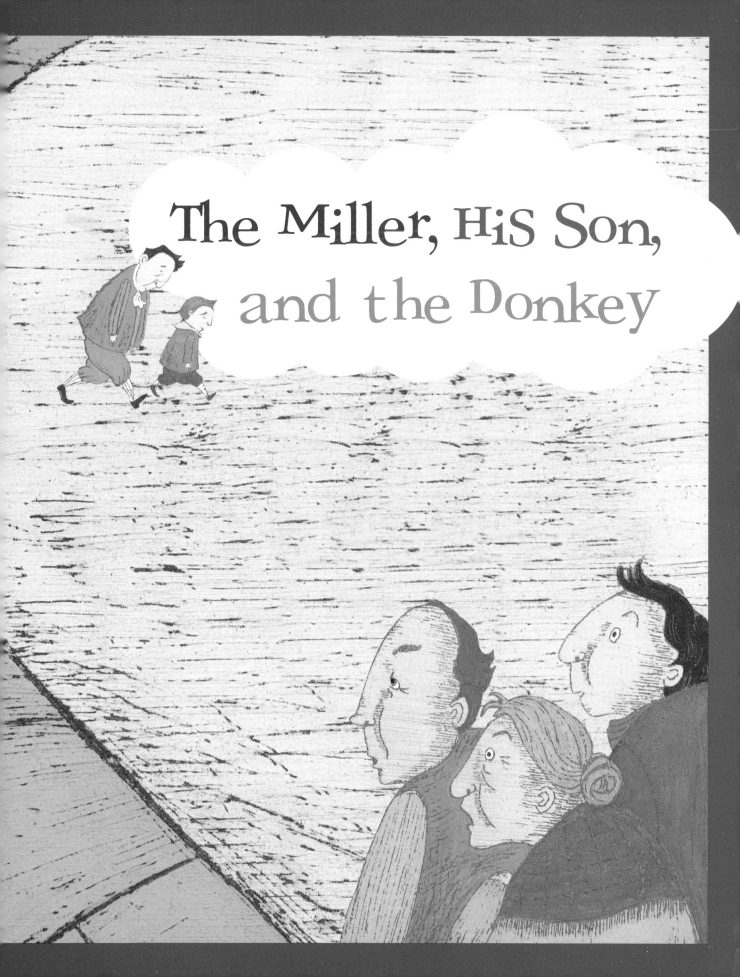

The Miller, His Son, and the Donkey

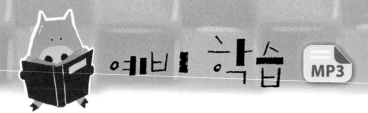

낱말 미리 보기

son
아들

market
시장

donkey
당나귀

meet
만나다

ride
타다

old
늙은

talk
이야기하다

father
아버지

women
여자들

wash
씻다

clothes
옷

town
읍

boy
소년

carry
운반하다

tie
묶다

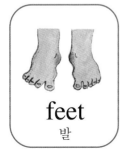
feet
발

pole
막대기

break
부서지다

catch
잡다

find
찾다

● **Look at that!**
저기 좀 봐.

● **How stupid!**
얼마나 어리석어!

● **He is right.**
그가 옳아.

● **You ride and I will walk.**
너는 타거라 나는 걷겠다.

● **Have you no respect?**
너는 존경심도 없니?

● **Get down!**
내려와!

● **Shame on you.**
부끄러운 줄 아세요.

● **Don't be cruel to the donkey!**
당나귀를 학대하지 마세요.

The Miller, His Son, and the Donkey

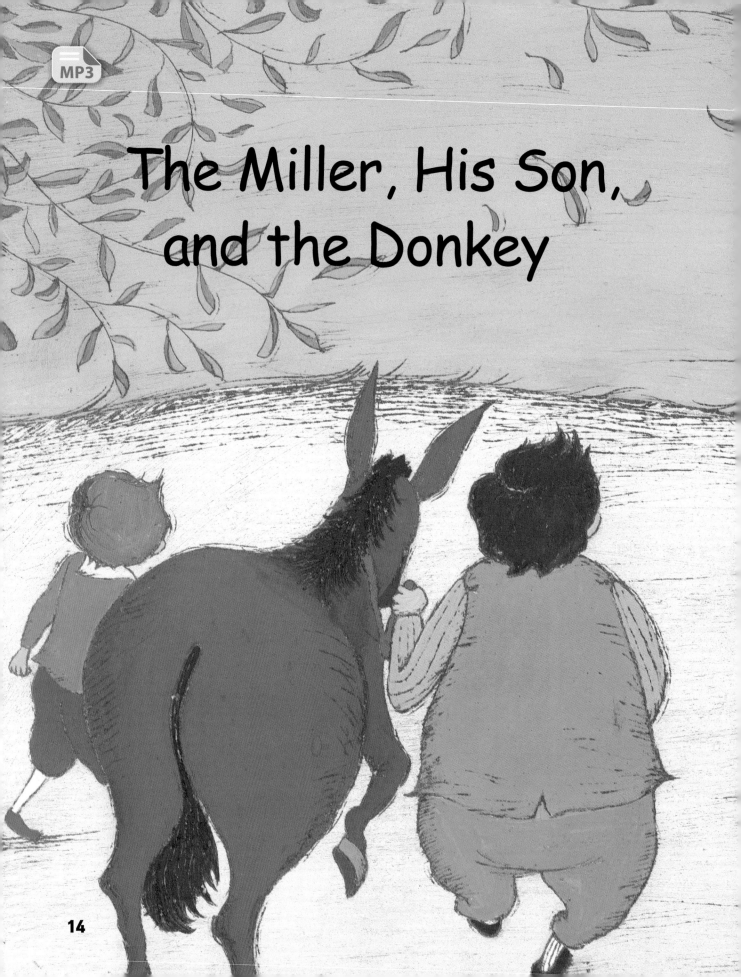

A miller and his **son** go to

the **market**.

They will sell their **donkey**.

On their way, they **meet** a man.

16

"Look at that!" the man says.

"They're not riding the **donkey**.

How stupid!"

The man laughs at them.

"He is right." says the miller.

He says to his **son**.

"You ride and I will walk."

So his **son rides** on the **donkey**.

And the miller walks.

Soon, they hear **old** people **talking.**

"A young man **ride**s while his **old**

father walks.

Have you no respect?

Get down, young man!"

The miller says to his **son**.

"Get down and let me **ride**."

So the miller **ride**s on the **donkey**.

And his **son** walks.

They pass by **women washing clothes**.

"Shame on you, **old** man," they shout.

"You should **ride** together with your **son**."

So they **ride** on the **donkey** together.

Soon, they come into the **town**.

A little **boy** looks at them and says,

"You two are riding on the **donkey** together!

Don't be cruel to the donkey!

You should **carry** the **donkey**."

So they **tie** the **donkey's**

feet to a **pole**.

And they **carry** the **donkey**.

But the **donkey** doesn't
like being carried.
So she tries to escape.

29

Finally the **donkey breaks** the **pole**.

Her **feet** are free.

Then the **donkey** runs away quickly.

The miller and his **son** try to **catch** her.

But they can't **catch** their **donkey**.

"Oh, no! Our **donkey**!"

They look for the **donkey**.

But they can't **find** her.

Finally they come back home without their **donkey**.

And they see how stupid they were.

낱말을 듣고, 따라 말하고, 따라 써보세요.

son [sʌn] 아들

son _____ _____

market [máːrkit] 시장

market _____ _____

donkey [dáŋki] 당나귀

donkey _____ _____

meet [miːt] 만나다

meet _____ _____

ride [raid] 타다

ride _____ _____

34

old [ould] 늙은

old _____ _____

talk [tɔːk] 이야기하다

talk _____ _____

father [fáːðər] 아버지

father _____ _____

women [wímin] 여자들

women _____ _____

wash [waʃ] 씻다

wash _____ _____

clothes [klouðz] 옷

clothes _____ _____

town [taun] 읍

town _____ _____

boy [bɔi] 소년

boy _____ _____

carry [kǽri] 운반하다

carry _____ _____

tie [tai] 묶다

tie _____ _____

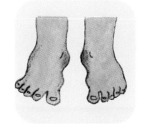

feet [fiːt] 발

feet

pole [poul] 막대기

pole

break [breik] 부서지다

break

catch [kætʃ] 잡다

catch

find [faind] 찾다

find

들려주는 낱말이 그림과 어울리면 ○표, 어울리지 않으면 ×표를 하세요.

그림에 알맞은 낱말을 보기에서 골라 말해보세요.

보기

son, father, pole, clothes, carry, feet, find

그림을 보고, 알맞은 낱말을 골라 동그라미하세요.

1
donkey | pole

2
son | clothes

3
tie | old

4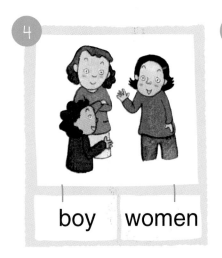
boy | women

5
carry | wash

6
ride | catch

7
meet | find

8
town | father

9
feet | talk

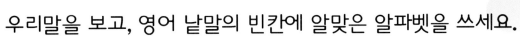

우리말을 보고, 영어 낱말의 빈칸에 알맞은 알파벳을 쓰세요.

1. 만나다 ☐ee☐

2. 소년 b☐y

3. 늙은 ol☐

4. 타다 r☐☐e

5. 옷 clo☐☐es

6. 여자들 ☐☐men

7. 묶다 ☐ie

8. 막대기 pol☐

9. 이야기하다 ta☐k

10. 발 ☐ee☐

11. 운반하다 c☐rr☐

12. 읍 tow☐

13. 부서지다 ☐reak

14. 아버지 fa☐☐er

15. 아들 s☐☐

16. 찾다 f☐nd

17. 잡다 cat☐☐

18. 당나귀 ☐on☐ey

19. 씻다 ☐ash

20. 시장 ma☐ke☐

41

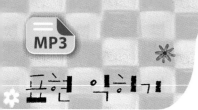

표현을 듣고, 따라 말하고, 따라 쓰세요.

- **Look at that!** 저기 좀 봐.

  Look at that!

  _____

- **How stupid!** 얼마나 어리석어!

  How stupid!

  _____

- **He is right.** 그가 옳아.

  He is right.

  _____

- **You ride and I will walk.** 너는 타거라 나는 걷겠다.

  You ride and I will walk.

  _____

- **Have you no respect?** 너는 존경심도 없니?

  Have you no respect?

  _____

Get down! 내려와!

<u>Get down!</u>

_____

Shame on you. 부끄러운 줄 아세요.

<u>Shame on you.</u>

_____

Don't be cruel to the donkey!

당나귀를 학대하지 마세요.

<u>Don't be cruel to the donkey!</u>

_____

✳ **감탄문의 표현**

'정말 예쁘다', '정말 크다'와 같이 자신의 느낌을 넣어서 표현하는 문장을 감탄문이라고 해요. 이런 문장은 보통 How로 시작하는데, How 다음에 자신의 느낌을 표현하는 낱말을 넣으면 감탄문이 돼요. 그리고 그 뒤에 주어와 동사를 넣어서 말할 수도 있답니다.

• How stupid (they are)!	(그들은) 얼마나 어리석은가!
• How pretty (she is)!	(그녀는) 얼마나 예쁜가!
• How tall he is!	그는 얼마나 키가 큰가!
• How cute the baby is!	그 아기는 얼마나 귀여운가!

그림을 보고, 알맞은 표현을 고르세요.

그림에 알맞은 표현을 보기에서 골라 말해보세요.

①

②

③

④

 그림에 어울리는 표현을 골라 동그라미하세요.

1. ① You should carry the donkey. ☐

   ② Don't be cruel to the donkey! ☐

2. ① You ride and I will walk. ☐

   ② He is right. ☐

3. ① Get down! ☐

   ② Shame on you. ☐

4. ① How stupid! ☐

   ② Look at that! ☐

뒤섞인 단어의 순서를 맞추어, 우리말에 맞는 표현을 쓰세요.

① 너는 타거라 나는 걷겠다. will walk you ride and I

→ _____

② 부끄러운 줄 아세요. on you shame

→ _____

③ 그가 옳아. is he right

→ _____

④ 너는 존경심도 없니? no respect you have

→ _____

⑤ 당나귀를 학대하지 마세요. be cruel to the donkey don't

→ _____

다른 가족과 친척의 이름은 영어로 뭐라고 할까요?

grandfather
할아버지

grandmother
할머니

mother
어머니

brothers
남자형제

sisters
여자형제

uncle
삼촌 / 외삼촌

aunt
고모 / 이모

cousin
사촌

nephew
남자조카

niece
여자조카

이럴 땐 이렇게 말해요.

Be careful!
조심해!

Hurry up!
서둘러!

Be quiet!
조용히 해!

Come in!
들어와!

Sit down!
앉아!

49

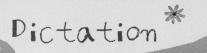
스토리를 들으면서 빈칸에 빠진 부분을 쓰세요.

A miller and his ❶_____ go to the ❷_____.

They will sell their donkey.

On their way, they ❸_____ a man.

" ④_____ " the man says.

"They're not riding the donkey.

⑤_____ "

The man laughs at them.

" ① _____ ," says the miller.

He says to his son,

" ② _____ "

So his son rides on the donkey.

And the miller walks.

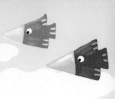

Soon, they hear ③ _____ people talking.

"A young man rides while his old ④ _____ walks.

⑤ _____

Get down, young man!"

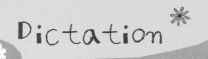

Dictation

The miller says to his son.

"① _____ and let me ride."

So the miller rides on the donkey.

And his son ② _____s.

They pass by ③ _____ washing clothes.

④ _____, old man," they shout.

"You should ⑤ _____ together with your son."

So they ride on the donkey together.

Soon, they come into the ① _____ .

A ② _____ boy looks at them and says,

"You two are riding on the donkey together!"

③ _____ to the donkey!

You should ④ _____ the donkey."

So they ⑤_____ the donkey's feet

to a ⑥_____.

And they carry the donkey.

But the donkey doesn't like being carried.

So she tries to escape.

Finally the donkey **①** _____s the pole.

Her **②** _____ are free.

Then the donkey runs away quickly.

The miller and his son try to **③** _____ her.

But they can't catch their donkey.

"Oh, no! Our ④_____!"

They look for the donkey.

But they can't ⑤_____ her.

Finally they come back home without their donkey.

And they see how stupid they were.

A 그림을 보고, 알맞은 문장에는 ○표를 하고, 틀린 문장에는 ✕표 하세요.

❶

① They come into the river. (   )

② A little boy looks at them and says. (   )

③ Don't be cruel to the lion! (   )

❷

① The donkey breaks the pole. (   )

② The donkey runs away quickly. (   )

③ But they can't catch the boy. (   )

B 그림의 내용을 가장 잘 표현한 문장을 고르세요.

 1

① They sell the donkey.

② They find the donkey.

③ They carry the donkey.

 2

① They hear boys talking.

② They hear women talking.

③ They hear old people talking.

C 그림의 내용을 보고, 빈칸에 알맞은 낱말을 보기에서 골라 쓰세요.

보기
find, son, meet, donkey, stupid

①

A miller and his ① _____ go to the market.
They will sell their ② _____ .
On their way, they ③ _____ a man.

②

They look for the donkey.
But they can't ① _____ her.
Finally they come back home without their donkey.
And they see how ② _____ they were.

D 주어진 표현을 이용하여 그림의 내용에 맞도록 문장을 쓰세요.

1.

그들은 축구하는 남자를 지나쳐가요.
(pass by / the man / they / playing football)

➜ _____

2.

토끼가 빨리 도망가요.
(runs away / quickly / the hare)

➜ _____

3.

그가 집을 부셔요.
(he / the house / breaks)

➜ _____

4.

나는 상자를 운반해야 해.
(carry / I / the box / should)

➜ _____

 이런 뜻이에요!

 예비학습

 듣기

 말하기

 읽기

 쓰기

The Ants and the Grasshopper

예비 학습 🎵 MP3

🌸 낱말 미리 보기

summer
여름

grass
잔디

green
녹색

hot
더운

ant
개미

collect
모으다

sweat
땀흘리다

under
~아래에

grasshopper
베짱이

sing
노래하다

shade
그늘

family
가족

winter
겨울

autumn
가을

crop
농작물

cold
추운

shake
떨다

visit
방문하다

give
주다

close
닫다

※ 표현 미리 보기

● **Why don't you sing with me?**
나와 함께 노래 부르지 않을래?

● **We are busy.**
우리는 바빠.

● **We must collect food.**
우리는 음식을 모아야 해.

● **There is lots of food.**
음식은 많이 있어.

● **It is summer now.**
지금은 여름이야.

● **Please let me in.**
나를 안으로 들어가게 해 줘.

● **Give me some food, please.**
저에게 음식 좀 주세요.

● **It's your own fault.**
그것은 순전히 너의 잘못이야.

The Ants
and the Grasshopper

It is a **summer** day.

The sun is shining.

The **grass** and the trees are **green**.

Fruits are here and there.

It is a **hot** afternoon.

But the **ant**s work hard.

They **collect** food.

They **sweat under** the sun.

But the **grasshopper sings**
in the **shade**.

"Why don't you sing with me?"
says the **grasshopper**.

"We are busy," says the **ant**.

"We must collect food for our **family**."

"There is lots of food,"

says the **grasshopper**.

"But there isn't any food in **winter**.

We must prepare for **winter**."

says the **ant**.

The **grasshopper** says,

"It is summer now.

Winter is so far away."

And the **grasshopper** enjoys **summer**.

Summer is over and **autumn** begins.

Crops are here and there.

The **grasshopper** eats the **crop**s.

He enjoys **autumn**.

But the **ant**s still work hard.

They gather the **crop**s.

And they store the **crop**s for **winter**.

Soon **winter** begins.

It is very **cold**.

And there isn't any food.

The **grasshopper shake**s with **cold**.

And he is very hungry.

The **grasshopper visit**s the **ant**s' house.

The **grasshopper** says,

"Please let me in.

And give me some food, please."

84

The **ant** says,

"We worked all **summer** and **autumn**.

But you didn't work at all.

It's your own fault."

And he **close**s the door.

The **grasshopper** regrets his laziness.

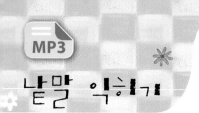

낱말을 듣고, 따라 말하고, 따라 써보세요.

summer [sʌ́mər] 여름

summer _____ _____

grass [græs] 잔디

grass _____ _____

green [griːn] 녹색

green _____ _____

hot [hat] 더운

hot _____ _____

ant [ænt] 개미

ant _____ _____

collect [kəlékt] 모으다

collect _____ _____

sweat [swet] 땀흘리다

sweat _____ _____

under [ʌ́ndər] ~ 아래에

under _____ _____

grasshopper [grǽshàpər] 베짱이

grasshopper _____ _____

sing [siŋ] 노래하다

sing _____ _____

shade [ʃeid] 그늘

shade

family [fǽməli] 가족

family

winter [wíntər] 겨울

winter

autumn [ɔ́:təm] 가을

autumn

crop [krɑp] 농작물

crop

cold [kould] 추운

cold

shake [ʃeik] 떨다

shake

visit [vízit] 방문하다

visit

give [giv] 주다

give

close [klouz] 닫다

close

들려주는 낱말에 맞는 그림을 골라 동그라미하세요.

①

②

③

④

⑤

⑥

그림에 알맞은 낱말을 보기에서 골라 말해보세요.

ant, sweat, hot, shade, grass, sing

필요 없는 글자에 X표하고, 올바른 낱말을 써 보세요.

1
carop

crop

2
hcold

3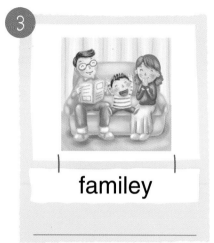
familey

4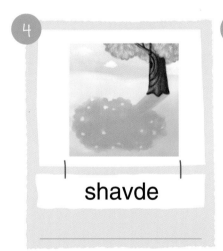
shavde

5
singz

6
viwsit

7
sumpmer

8
cblose

9
givje

가로와 세로 열쇠를 보고, 낱말퍼즐을 풀어보세요.

가로열쇠 ② 겨울 ⑥ 농작물 ⑦ 개미 ⑩ 닫다 ⑫ 녹색 ⑮ 더운 ⑯ 베짱이 ⑱ 방문하다 ⑲ ~ 아래에 ⑳ 가족

세로열쇠 ① 땀흘리다 ③ 그늘 ④ 모으다 ⑤ 주다 ⑧ 여름 ⑨ 잔디 ⑪ 노래하다 ⑬ 떨다 ⑭ 추운 ⑰ 가을

①↓ s

②→ w

③↓ s

④↓ c

⑤↓ g

⑥→ c

⑦→ a

⑧↓ s

⑨↓ g

⑩→ c

⑪↓ s

⑫→ g

⑬↓ s

⑭↓ c

⑮→ h

⑯→ g

⑰↓ a

⑱→ v

⑲→ u

⑳→ f

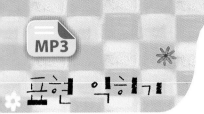

표현 익히기 표현을 듣고, 따라 말하고, 따라 쓰세요.

● **Why don't you sing with me?** 나와 함께 노래 부르지 않을래?

Why don't you sing with me?

_____

● **We are busy.** 우리는 바빠.

We are busy.

_____

● **We must collect food.** 우리는 음식을 모아야 해.

We must collect food.

_____

● **There is lots of food.** 음식은 많이 있어.

There is lots of food.

_____

● **It is summer now.** 지금은 여름이야.

It is summer now.

_____

96

Please let me in.
나를 안으로 들어가게 해 줘.

Please let me in.

_____

Give me some food, please. 저에게 음식 좀 주세요.

Give me some food, please.

_____

It's your own fault. 그것은 순전히 너의 잘못이야.

It's your own fault.

_____

 의무의 표현

'~해야 한다'를 표현할 때는 동사 앞에 must를 써서 표현해요. must 뒤에 이어지는 동사는 항상 원형을 쓰고요.

- We must collect food.   우리는 음식을 모아야 해
- We must study hard.   우리는 열심히 공부해야 해.
- We must clean our room today.   우리는 오늘 방 청소를 해야 해.

97

들려주는 표현이 어울리는 그림을 골라 순서대로 번호를 쓰세요.

그림에 알맞은 표현을 보기에서 골라 말해보세요.

보기

Please let me in.　　We must collect food.

We are busy.　　Give me some food, please.

1

2

3

4

그림과 문장이 서로 어울리도록 연결하세요.

①

②

③

④

⑤

- We are busy.

- We must collect food.

- There is lots of food.

- Give me some food, please.

- Please let me in.

우리말 표현을 보고, 밑줄 친 부분에 들어갈 낱말을 골라 쓰세요.

① 음식은 많이 있어.

→ There is lots of _____ .

□ family
□ food

② 지금은 여름이야.

→ It is _____ now.

□ winter
□ summer

③ 나와 함께 노래 부르지 않을래?

→ Why don't you _____ with me?

□ close
□ sing

④ 우리는 음식을 모아야 해.

→ We must _____ food.

□ collect
□ work

⑤ 저에게 음식 좀 주세요.

→ _____ me some food, please.

□ Give
□ Visit

뽀너스 뽀너스!

다른 곤충의 이름은 뭐라고 할까요?

bee
벌

mosquito
모기

fly
파리

spider
거미

butterfly
나비

ladybug
무당벌레

dragonfly
잠자리

beetle
딱정벌레

firefly
개똥벌레

cricket
귀뚜라미

이럴 땐 이렇게 말해요.

Why don't you take a walk together?
함께 산책하지 않을래?

Why don't you swim together?
함께 수영하지 않을래?

Why don't you play tennis together?
함께 테니스 치지 않을래?

Why don't you study together?
함께 공부하지 않을래?

Why don't you play the piano together?
함께 피아노 연주하지 않을래?

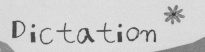

It is a ❶ _____ day.

The sun is shining.

The ❷ _____ and the trees are ❸ _____.

Fruits are here and there.

It is a ④ _____ afternoon.

But the ants work hard.

They ⑤ _____ food.

They sweat ⑥ _____ the sun.

But the grasshopper sings in the ① _____.

"Why don't you ② _____ with me?"

says the grasshopper.

" ③ _____ ," says the ant.

" ④ _____ for our family."

" ⑤_____,"

says the grasshopper.

"But there isn't any food in winter.

We must prepare for ⑥_____"

says the ⑦_____.

MP3

The grasshopper says,

" ① _____

② _____ is so far away."

And the grasshopper enjoys ③ _____.

Summer is over and ④ _____ begins.

⑤ _____s are here and there.

The ⑥ _____ eats the crops.

He enjoys autumn.

But the ❶ _____ s still work hard.

They gather the ❷ _____ s.

And they store the crops for ❸ _____ .

Soon winter begins.

It is very ④_____.

And there isn't any ⑤_____.

The grasshopper ⑥_____s with cold.

And he is very ⑦_____.

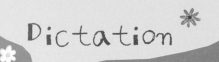

The grasshopper ①_____s the ants' house.

The grasshopper says,

"②_____

And ③_____."

The ant ④_____s.

"We worked all ⑤_____ and autumn.
But you didn't work at all.

⑥_____"

And they ⑦_____s the door.
The grasshopper regrets his laziness.

A 그림을 보고, 알맞은 문장에는 ○표를 하고, 틀린 문장에는 ✕표 하세요.

1

① It is a cold winter. (   )

② The ants work hard. (   )

③ They sing under the sun. (   )

2

① Soon autumn begins. (   )

② There isn't any food. (   )

③ The grasshopper shakes with cold. (   )

B 그림의 내용을 가장 잘 표현한 문장을 고르세요.

① The trees are red.

② The sun is shining.

③ There isn't any fruit.

① The ants eat crops.

② The grasshopper eats the fruit.

③ The grasshopper eats the crops.

C 그림의 내용을 보고, 빈칸에 알맞은 낱말을 보기에서 골라 쓰세요.

보기 family, winter, collect, ant, crop, shade

①

But the grasshopper sings in the ❶_____.

"Why don't you sing with me?" says the grasshopper.

"We are busy," says the ant.

We must ❷_____ food for our ❸_____.

②

But the ❶_____s still work hard.

They gather the ❷_____s.

And they store the crops for ❸_____.

D 주어진 표현을 이용하여 그림의 내용에 맞도록 문장을 쓰세요.

①

그들은 과일을 먹는다.
(fruits / they / eat)

➜ _____

②

우유가 많이 있다.
(lots of / is / milk / there)

➜ _____

③

나는 저녁을 준비하고 있다.
(dinner / I / prepare for)

➜ _____

④

개가 의자 아래에 있다.
(the chair / under / is / the dog)

➜ _____

 이런 뜻이에요!

예비 학습	듣기	말하기	읽기	쓰기

The Honest Woodcutter

예비 학습 🎵 MP3

🌸 낱말 미리 보기

woodcutter
나무꾼

tall
키가 큰

ax
도끼

bird
새

slip
미끄러지다

fall
빠지다

river
강

cry
울다

beautiful
아름다운

nymph
요정

help
돕다

dive
뛰어들다

hold
잡다

gold
금

silver
은

this
이것

iron
쇠

that
저것

smile
미소 짓다

three
셋의

※ 표현 미리 보기

● **Why are you crying?**
너는 왜 울고 있니?

● **My family will be hungry.**
나의 가족은 굶게 될 거야.

● **I can help you.**
나는 너를 도와줄 수 있어.

● **Will you wait a moment, please?**
잠시만 기다려 줄래?

● **I will wait here.**
나는 여기서 기다릴 거야.

● **Is this yours?**
이거 네 거니?

● **My ax is made of iron.**
내 도끼는 쇠로 만든 거야.

● **That is my ax.**
저것이 내 도끼야.

The Honest Woodcutter

A **woodcutter** goes to the woods.

He cuts a **tall** tree with his **ax**.

He hears **bird**s singing.

He sees the **birds**.

And then his **ax slips**.

The **ax falls** into the **river**.

"Oh, no! This is my only **ax**.

Now I don't have an **ax**.

So I can't cut any trees."

He cries and cries.

After a while,
he hears a **beautiful** voice.
"Excuse me.
Why are you crying?"
asks the **nymph**.

"I dropped my **ax** into the **river**,"
says the **woodcutter**.
"Without it, I can't cut any trees.
Then my family will be hungry."

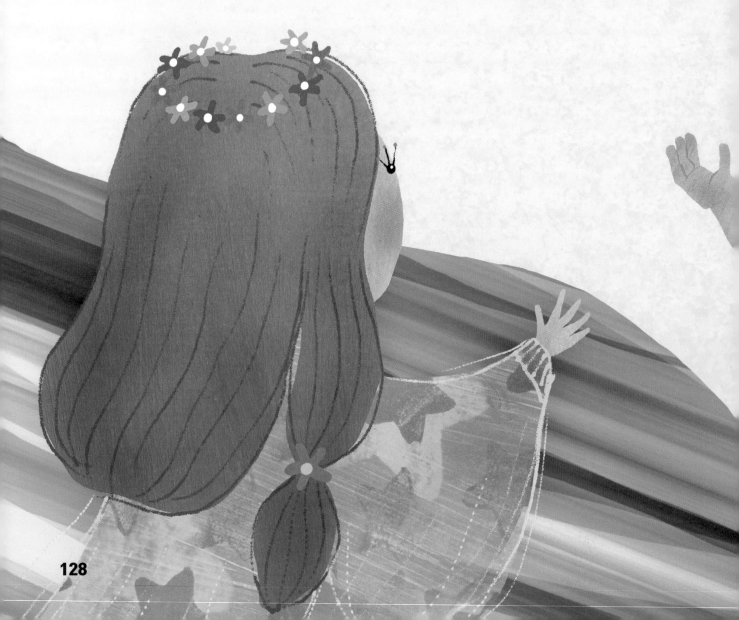

128

"I can help you," says the **nymph.**

"Will you wait a moment, please?"

"Sure. I will wait here,"

says the **woodcutter.**

The **nymph dives** into the **river.**

After a while, she appears again.

She is **hold**ing a **gold ox**.

"Is this yours?" asks the **nymph**.

"No, it isn't," says the **woodcutter**.

"My **ax** isn't made of **gold**,"
says the **woodcutter**.
The **nymph dive**s again.

And she appears with a **silver ax.**

"Is this yours?" asks the nymph.

"No. My ax is made of iron."

says the **woodcutter.**

137

This time,
she appears with an **iron ax**.
"That is my ax!"
shouts the **woodcutter**.
"Thank you, I'm so happy."

The **nymph smile**s.

"You are a very honest man.

I'll give you these **gold** and **silver axe**s."

"Oh, thank you so much."

He goes back home with his **three axe**s.

낱말 익히기 낱말을 듣고, 따라 말하고, 따라 써보세요.

woodcutter [wúdkʌ̀tər] 나무꾼

woodcutter _____ _____

tall [tɔːl] 키가 큰

tall _____ _____

ax [æks] 도끼

ax _____ _____

bird [bəːrd] 새

bird _____ _____

slip [slip] 미끄러지다

slip _____ _____

142

fall [fɔːl] 빠지다

fall _____ _____

river [rívər] 강

river _____ _____

cry [krai] 울다

cry _____ _____

beautiful [bjúːtəfəl] 아름다운

beautiful _____ _____

nymph [nimf] 요정

nymph _____ _____

help [help] 돕다

help _____ _____

dive [daiv] 뛰어들다

dive _____ _____

hold [hould] 잡다

hold _____ _____

gold [gould] 금

gold _____ _____

silver [sílvər] 은

silver _____ _____

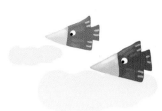

this [ðis] 이것

this

iron [áiərn] 쇠

iron

that [ðæt] 저것

that

smile [smail] 미소 짓다

smile

three [θriː] 셋의

three

그림을 보고, 알맞은 영어 낱말을 고르세요.

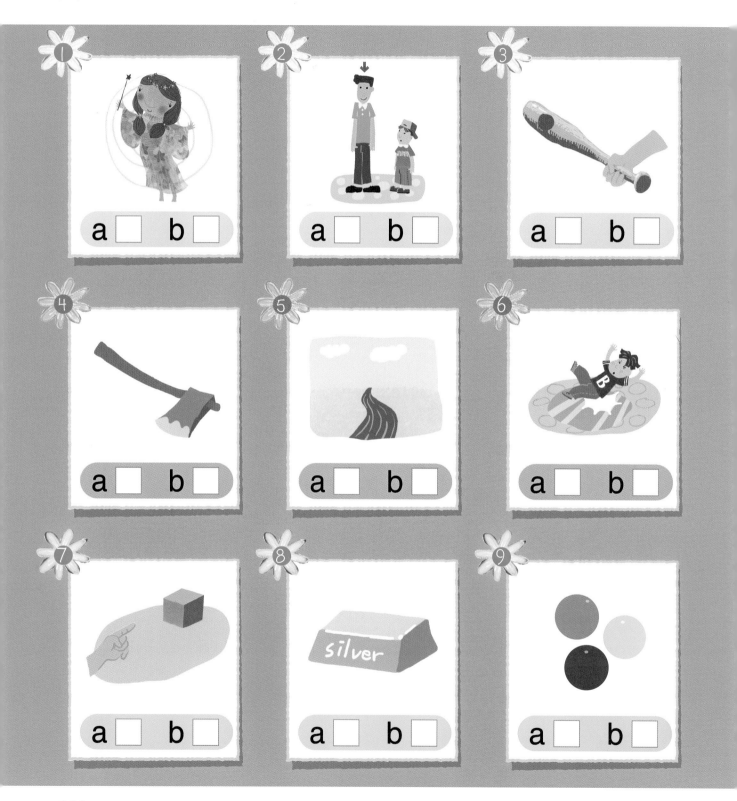

그림에 알맞은 낱말을 보기에서 골라 말해보세요.

tall, smile, slip, bird, cry, hold, three

1.
2.
3.
4.
5.
6.
7.

그림을 보고 알맞은 낱말을 골라 동그라미하세요.

1	2	3
lion iron	dive daiv	cry crs

4	5	6
helf help	bird burd	feel fall

7	8	9
ax au	beautiful beutipul	thiz this

우리말 뜻에는 영어 낱말을 쓰고, 영어 낱말에는 우리말 뜻을 쓰세요.

① 셋의　　t_____　　② fall　　_____

③ 금　　g_____　　④ river　　_____

⑤ 요정　　n_____　　⑥ smile　　_____

⑦ 뛰어들다　d_____　⑧ tall　　_____

⑨ 은　　s_____　　⑩ hold　　_____

⑪ 이것　　t_____　　⑫ beautiful　_____

⑬ 도끼　　a_____　　⑭ cry　　_____

⑮ 저것　　t_____　　⑯ slip　　_____

⑰ 쇠　　i_____　　⑱ woodcutter _____

⑲ 돕다　　h_____　　⑳ bird　　_____

표현 익히기   표현을 듣고, 따라 말하고, 따라 쓰세요.

Why are you crying?
너는 왜 울고 있니?

Why are you crying?

_____

My family will be hungry. 나의 가족은 굶게 될 거야.

My family will be hungry.

_____

I can help you. 나는 널 도와줄 수 있어.

I can help you.

_____

Will you wait a moment, please? 잠시만 기다려 줄래?

Will you wait a moment, please?

_____

I will wait here. 나는 여기서 기다릴 거야.

I will wait here.

_____

● **Is this yours?** 이거 네 거니?

Is this yours?

_____

_____

● **My ax is made of iron.** 내 도끼는 쇠로 만든 거야.

My ax is made of iron.

_____

_____

● **That is my ax.** 저것이 내 도끼야.

That is my ax.

_____

_____

---

 be made of / be made from

' ~으로 만든 ' 이라는 표현을 할 때, be made of 또는 be made from을 사용해요. 재료의 형태를 보존하고 있을 때는 be made of를 쓰고, 재료의 형태를 알 수 없게 되었을 경우에는 be made from을 쓴답니다.

- My ax is made of iron.   내 도끼는 쇠로 만든 것이다.
- The table is made of wood.   그 식탁은 나무로 만든 것이다.
- Cheese is made from milk.   치즈는 우유로 만든 것이다.
- Wine is made from grapes.   포도주는 포도로 만든 것이다.

들려주는 표현 중에서 어울리는 그림을 골라 (a) 또는 (b)를 쓰세요.

1

2

3

152

그림에 알맞은 표현을 보기에서 골라 말해보세요.

보기
Will you wait a moment, please?
I will wait here.   Why are you crying?

1

2

그림에 어울리는 표현을 골라 동그라미하세요.

① I can help you. ☐

② I will wait here. ☐

① Is this yours? ☐

② That is my ax. ☐

① Will you wait a moment, please? ☐

② Why are you crying? ☐

① My family will be hungry. ☐

② I can't cut any trees. ☐

154

뒤섞인 표현의 순서를 맞추어, 우리말에 맞게 완성하세요.

① 나는 여기서 기다릴 거야. wait   I   here   will

→ _____

② 나의 가족은 굶게 될 거야. will be   my family   hungry

→ _____

③ 내 도끼는 쇠로 만든 거야. my ax   made of iron   is

→ _____

④ 나는 널 도와줄 수 있어. help   I   you   can

→ _____

⑤ 저것이 내 도끼야. is   that   my ax

→ _____

155

다른 행동들은 영어로 뭐라고 할까요?

drive
운전하다

kick
차다

draw
그림을 그리다

study
공부하다

read
읽다

cook
요리하다

swim
수영하다

drink
마시다

jump
뛰다

wash
씻다

이럴 땐 이렇게 말해요.

I can read a book.

나는 책을 읽을 수 있어.

I can't read a book.

나는 책을 읽을 수 없어.

I can swim in the sea.

나는 바다에서 수영할 수 있어.

I can't swim in the sea.

나는 바다에서 수영할 수 없어.

I can jump high.

나는 높이 뛸 수 있어.

I can't jump high.

나는 높이 뛸 수 없어.

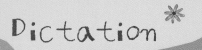

A woodcutter goes to the woods.

He cuts a ① _____ tree with his ax.

He hears ② _____ singing.

He sees the birds.

And then his ax ③ _____s.

The ax ④_____ s into the ⑤_____.

"Oh, no! This is my only ⑥_____.

Now I don't have an ax.

So I can't ⑦_____ any trees."

He cries and cries.

After a while,

he hears a ❶ _____ voice.

"Excuse me.

❷ _____" asks the nymph.

"I dropped my ax into the river."

says the ③_____.

"Without it, I can't cut any ④_____s."

Then ⑤_____."

MP3

" ① _____," says the nymph.

"Will you wait a moment, please?"

"Sure. ② _____,"

says the woodcutter.

The nymph ③ _____s into the river.

After a while, she appears again.

She is holding a ④ _____ ax.

" ⑤ _____ " asks the nymph.

"No, it isn't," says the woodcutter.

"My ax isn't made of ❶_____."

says the woodcutter.

The nymph ❷_____s again.

And she appears with a ③_____ ax.

"Is this yours?" asks the ④_____ .

"No. ⑤_____,"

says the ⑥_____ .

This time, she appears with an ❶ _____ ax.

"❷ _____"

shouts the woodcutter.

"Thank you, I'm so happy."

The nymph ③_____s.

"You are a very honest ④_____.

I'll ⑤_____ you these gold and silver axes."

"Oh, thank you so much."

He goes back home with his ⑥_____ axes.

A 그림을 보고, 알맞은 문장에는 ○표를 하고, 틀린 문장에는 ✕표 하세요.

①

① A nymph goes to the woods. (   )

② He cuts a tall tree with his ax. (   )

③ He hears birds singing. (   )

②

① The nymph appears with an iron ax. (   )

② "That is my bird!" shouts the woodcutter. (   )

③ "Thank you, I'm so angry." (   )

B 그림의 내용을 가장 잘 표현한 문장을 고르세요.

1

① The ax falls into the river.

② The ax falls into the grass.

③ The ax falls into the woods.

2

① She is holding a gold ax.

② She is holding a silver ax.

③ She is holding an iron ax.

C 그림의 내용을 보고, 빈칸에 알맞은 내용을 보기에서 골라 쓰세요.

보기 help, nymph, iron, wait, silver, woodcutter

①

"I can ❶ _____ you," says the nymph.

"Will you wait a moment, please?"

"Sure. I will ❷ _____ here," says the ❸ _____.

②

And she appears with a ❶ _____ ax.

"Is this yours?" asks the ❷ _____.

"No. My ax is made of ❸ _____."

D 주어진 표현을 이용하여 그림의 내용에 맞도록 문장을 쓰세요.

그녀는 새가 노래하는 소리를 듣는다.
(singing / hears / she / birds)

➜

나는 풍선을 가지고 집으로 돌아온다.
(home / I / with a balloon / go back)

➜

책이 강에 빠진다.
(falls into / the river / the book)

➜ _____

나는 그녀에게 연필을 준다.
(I / her / a pencil / give)

➜ _____

The Miller, His Son, and the Donkey

⟨14p-15p⟩

A miller and his son go to the market.
They will sell their donkey.
On their way, they meet a man.

방앗간 주인과 그의 아들이 시장에 가요.
그들은 당나귀를 팔려고 해요.
길을 가던 중에 한 남자를 만나요.

⟨16p-17p⟩

"Look at that!" the man says.
"They're not riding the donkey.
How stupid!"
The man laughs at them.

"저것 좀 봐." 남자는 말해요.
"저 사람들은 당나귀를 타지 않네.
얼마나 어리석어!"
남자는 그들을 비웃어요.

⟨18p-19p⟩

"He is right," says the miller.
He says to his son,
"You ride and I will walk."
So his son rides on the donkey.
And the miller walks.

"그가 옳아." 방앗간 주인이 말해요.
그는 그의 아들에게 말해요.
"너는 올라 타거라, 나는 걷겠다."
그래서 그의 아들은 당나귀를 타요.
그리고 방앗간 주인은 걸어요.

⟨20p-21p⟩

Soon, they hear old people talking.
"A young man rides while his old father walks.
Have you no respect?
Get down, young man!"

곧 그들은 노인들이 말하는 것을 들어요.
"늙은 아버지는 걸어가는데 젊은이가 타고 가네.
너는 존경심도 없느냐?
내려오게, 젊은이!"

⟨22p-23p⟩

The miller says to his son.
"Get down and let me ride."
So the miller rides on the donkey.
And his son walks.

방앗간 주인은 그의 아들에게 말해요.
"내려와라, 내가 올라타마."
그래서 방앗간 주인이 당나귀를 타요.
그리고 그의 아들은 걸어요.

<24p-25p>

They pass by women washing clothes.
"Shame on you, old man," they shout.
"You should ride together with your son."
So they ride on the donkey together.

그들은 옷을 빨고 있는 여자들 옆을 지나가요.
"부끄러운 줄 아세요, 노인양반," 그들은 소리쳐요.
"당신의 아들과 함께 타야죠."
그래서 그들은 함께 당나귀를 타요.

<26p-27p>

Soon, they come into town.
A little boy looks at them and says,
"You two are riding on the donkey together!
Don't be cruel to the donkey!
You should carry the donkey."

곧, 그들은 읍으로 들어가요.
한 작은 소년이 그들을 보고 말해요.
"당신들 둘이서 당나귀를 함께 타고 가네요!
당나귀를 학대하지 마세요!
당신들은 당나귀를 들고 가야 해요."

<28p-29p>

So they tie the donkey's feet to a pole.
And they carry the donkey.
But the donkey doesn't like being carried.
So she tries to escape.

그래서 그들은 당나귀의 발을 막대기에 묶어요.
그리고 그들은 당나귀를 들고 가요.
그러나 당나귀는 들려서 가는 것을 좋아하지 않아요.
그래서 빠져나가려고 해요.

<30p-31p>

Finally the donkey breaks the pole.
Her feet are free.
Then the donkey runs away quickly.
The miller and his son try to catch her.
But they can't catch their donkey.

마침내 당나귀는 막대기를 부러뜨려요.
당나귀의 발이 자유로워요.
그러자 당나귀는 재빨리 도망가 버려요.
방앗간 주인과 그의 아들은 당나귀를 잡으려고 해요.
그러나 그들은 당나귀를 잡을 수 없어요.

<32p-33p>

"Oh, no! Our donkey!"
They look for the donkey.
But they can't find her.
Finally they come back home without their donkey.
And they see how stupid they were.

"오, 안돼! 우리 당나귀!"
그들은 당나귀를 찾아봐요.
그러나 그들은 찾을 수 없어요.
마침내 그들은 당나귀 없이 집으로 돌아가요.

그리고 그들은 자신들이 얼마나 어리석었는지 알게 된답니다.

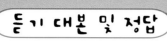

낱말 익히기

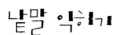 듣기 문제 ·················· 38p

(듣기대본)

❶ father ❷ catch ❸ market
❹ ride ❺ women ❻ break
❼ meet ❽ wash ❾ talk

정답

❶ ○   ❷ ×   ❸ ○
❹ ○   ❺ ×   ❻ ×
❼ ○   ❽ ○   ❾ ×

말하기 문제 ·················· 39p

❶ father ❷ son ❸ carry ❹ find
❺ clothes ❻ pole ❼ feet

읽기 문제 ·················· 40p

❶ donkey ❷ son ❸ old
❹ women ❺ carry ❻ catch
❼ find ❽ town ❾ talk

쓰기 문제 ·················· 41p

❶ m e e t   ❷ b o y
❸ o l d   ❹ r i d e
❺ c l o t h e s   ❻ w o m e n
❼ t i e   ❽ p o l e
❾ t a l k   ❿ f e e t

⑪ c a r r y   ⑫ t o w n
⑬ b r e a k   ⑭ f a t h e r
⑮ s o n   ⑯ f i n d
⑰ c a t c h   ⑱ d o n k e y
⑲ w a s h   ⑳ m a r k e t

표현 익히기

듣기 문제 ·················· 44p

(듣기대본)

❶ (a) Get down!
   (b) How stupid!

❷ (a) Don't be cruel to the donkey!
   (b) He is right.

❸ (a) Shame on you.
   (b) You ride and I will walk.

❹ (a) Have you no respect?
   (b) He is right.

❺ (a) How stupid!
   (b) Look at that!

정답

❶ (a)   ❷ (a)   ❸ (b)   ❹ (a)   ❺ (b)

말하기 문제 45p

① Look at that!
② Have you no respect?
③ Get down.
④ You ride and I will walk.

읽기 문제 46p

①② ②① ③① ④②

쓰기 문제 47p

① You ride and I will walk.
② Shame on you.
③ He is right.
④ Have you no respect?
⑤ Don't be cruel to the donkey!

Dictation

50p-51p

① son ② market ③ meet
④ Look at that! ⑤ How stupid!

52p-53p

① He is right. ② You ride and I will walk.
③ old   ④ father
⑤ Have you no respect?

54p-55p

① Get down ② walk ③ women
④ Shame on you.   ⑤ ride

56p-57p

① town ② little ③ Don't be cruel
④ carry ⑤ tie ⑥ pole

58p-59p

① break   ② feet ③ catch
④ donkey ⑤ find

스토리 이해하기 60p-63p

A ① ① × ② ○ ③ ×
  ② ① ○ ② ○ ③ ×

B ① ③   ② ③

C ① ① son ② donkey ③ meet
  ② ① find ② stupid

D ① They pass by the man playing
     football.
  ② The hare runs away quickly.
  ③ He breaks the house.
  ④ I should carry the box.

The Ants and the Grasshopper

〈68p-69p〉

It is a summer day. The sun is shining. The grass and the trees are green. Fruits are here and there.	여름날이에요. 해가 빛나고 있어요. 잔디와 나무들은 푸르러요. 과일들이 여기저기에 있어요.

〈70p-71p〉

It is a hot afternoon. But the ants work hard. They collect food. They sweat under the sun.	무더운 오후예요. 그러나 개미들은 열심히 일해요. 그들은 음식을 모아요. 그들은 태양 아래에서 땀을 흘려요.

〈72p-73p〉

But the grasshopper sings in the shade. "Why don't you sing with me?" says the grasshopper. "We are busy," says the ant. "We must collect food for our family."	그러나 베짱이는 그늘에서 노래를 불러요. "나랑 같이 노래 부르지 않을래?" 베짱이가 말해요. "우리는 바빠." 개미는 말해요. "우리는 가족을 위해 음식을 모아야 해."

〈74p-75p〉

"There is lots of food," says the grasshopper. "But there isn't any food in winter. We must prepare for winter." says the ant.	"음식은 많이 있어." 베짱이가 말해요. "그러나 겨울에는 음식이 없어. 우리는 겨울을 대비해서 준비를 해야만 해." 개미가 말해요.

〈76p-77p〉

The grasshopper says, "It is summer now. Winter is so far away." And the grasshopper enjoys summer.	베짱이가 말해요. "지금은 여름이야. 겨울이 오려면 아직도 멀었어." 그리고 베짱이는 여름을 즐겨요.

176

〈78p-79p〉

Summer is over and autumn begins.
Crops are here and there.
The grasshopper eats the crops.
He enjoys autumn.

여름이 끝나고 가을이 시작돼요.
농작물들이 여기저기 있어요.
베짱이는 농작물을 먹어요.
그는 가을을 즐겨요.

〈80p-81p〉

But the ants still work hard.
They gather the crops.
And they store the crops for winter.

그러나 개미들은 여전히 열심히 일해요.
그들은 농작물을 모아요.
그리고 그들은 겨울을 대비해서 농작물들을 저장해요.

〈82p-83p〉

Soon winter begins.
It is very cold.
And there isn't any food.
The grasshopper shakes with cold.
And he is very hungry.

곧 겨울이 시작돼요.
날씨가 아주 추워요.
그리고 음식이 전혀 없어요.
베짱이는 추워서 떨어요.
그리고 그는 배가 몹시 고파요.

〈84p-85p〉

The grasshopper visits the ants' house.
The grasshopper says,
"Please let me in.
 And give me some food, please."

베짱이는 개미의 집을 방문해요.
베짱이는 말해요.
"나 좀 들어가게 해 줘.
 그리고 나에게 음식 좀 줘."

〈86p-87p〉

The ant says,
"We worked all summer and autumn.
 But you didn't work at all.
 It's your own fault."
And he closes the door.
The grasshopper regrets his laziness.

개미가 말해요.
"우리는 여름과 가을 내내 일했어.
 그러나 너는 전혀 일을 하지 않았어.
 그건 네 잘못이야."
그리고 그는 문을 닫아요.
베짱이는 자신의 게으름을 후회해요.

낱말 익히기

🐸 듣기 문제 ································· 92p

(듣기대본)

① hot ② autumn ③ shake
④ sing ⑤ under ⑥ ant

정답 ·······················

① 두번째 그림 ② 두번째 그림 ③ 첫번째 그림
④ 두번째 그림 ⑤ 두번째 그림 ⑥ 첫번째 그림

🐀 말하기 문제 ·······················93p

① sweat ② sing ③ hot
④ shade ⑤ grass ⑥ ant

📖 읽기 문제 ························· 94p

① crop ② cold ③ family
④ shade ⑤ sing ⑥ visit
⑦ summer ⑧ close ⑨ give

🏠 쓰기 문제 ·················· 95p

① sweat ② winter ③ shade
④ collect ⑤ give ⑥ crop
⑦ ant ⑧ summer ⑨ grass
⑩ close ⑪ sing ⑫ green
⑬ shake ⑭ cold ⑮ hot
⑯ grasshopper ⑰ autumn
⑱ visit ⑲ under ⑳ family

표현 익히기

🐸 듣기 문제 ····························· 98p

(듣기대본)

① There is lots of food.
② Please let me in.
③ We are busy.
④ Give me some food, please.
⑤ We must collect food.

정답 ·······················

5, 1
4, 3
2

🐀 말하기 문제 ·····················99p

① Give me some food, please.
② We are busy.
③ Please let me in.
④ We must collect food.

📖 읽기 문제 ·····················100p

① There is lots of food.
② Give me some food, please.
③ Please let me in.
④ We are busy.
⑤ We must collect food.

🦓 쓰기 문제 ·················· 101p

❶ food   ❷ summer   ❸ sing

❹ collect   ❺ Give

Dictation

104p-105p

❶ summer   ❷ grass   ❸ green

❹ hot   ❺ collect   ❻ under

106p-107p

❶ shade   ❷ sing   ❸ We are busy

❹ We must collect food

❺ There is lots of food

❻ winter   ❼ ant

108p-109p

❶ It is summer now.   ❷ Winter

❸ summer   ❹ autumn   ❺ Crop

❻ grasshopper

110p-111p

❶ ant   ❷ crop   ❸ winter   ❹ cold

❺ food   ❻ shake   ❼ hungry

112p-113p

❶ visit   ❷ Please let me in.

❸ give me some food, please

❹ say   ❺ summer

❻ It's your own fault.

❼ close

스토리 이해하기 ········ 114p-117p

A ❶ ① ×   ② ○   ③ ×
    ❷ ① ×   ② ○   ③ ○

B ❶ ②   ❷ ③

C ❶ ① shade   ② collect   ③ family
    ❷ ① ant   ② crop   ③ winter

D ❶ They eat fruits.
    ❷ There is lots of milk.
    ❸ I prepare for dinner.
    ❹ The dog is under the chair.

The Honest Woodcutter

〈122p-123p〉

A woodcutter goes to the woods.
He cuts a tall tree with his ax.
He hears birds singing.
He sees the birds.
And then his ax slips.

나무꾼은 숲에 가요.
그는 도끼로 큰 나무를 베요.
그는 새들이 노래하는 소리를 들어요.
그는 새들을 봐요.
그리고 그때 그의 도끼가 미끄러져요.

〈124p-125p〉

The ax falls into the river.
"Oh, no! This is my only ax.
 Now I don't have an ax.
 So I can't cut any trees."
He cries and cries.

도끼가 강물 속으로 빠져요.
"오, 안돼! 이건 나의 유일한 도끼인데."
 이제 나는 도끼가 없어.
 그래서 나무를 벨 수가 없어.
그는 울고 또 울어요.

〈126p-127p〉

After a while, he hears a beautiful voice.
"Excuse me.
 Why are you crying?" asks the nymph.

잠시 후에, 그는 아름다운 목소리를 들어요.
"실례합니다.
 당신은 왜 울고 있나요?" 요정이 물어요.

〈128p-129p〉

"I dropped my ax into the river,"
says the woodcutter.
"Without it, I can't cut any trees.
 Then my family will be hungry."

"제 도끼를 강물에 떨어뜨렸어요."
나무꾼이 말해요.
"그것이 없이는 나무를 벨 수가 없어요.
 그러면 제 가족은 굶주리게 될 거예요."

〈130p-131p〉

"I can help you," says the nymph.
"Will you wait a moment, please?"
"Sure. I will wait here,"
says the woodcutter.
The nymph dives into the river.

"제가 당신을 도울 수 있어요." 요정이 말해요.
"잠시만 기다려 주시겠어요?"
"물론이죠. 여기서 기다릴게요."
나무꾼이 말해요.
요정은 물속으로 뛰어들어요.

〈132p-133p〉

After a while, she appears again.
She is holding a gold ax.
"Is this yours?" asks the nymph.
"No, it isn't," says the woodcutter.

잠시 후, 그녀는 다시 나타나요.
그녀는 금도끼를 들고 있어요.
"이것이 당신의 것인가요?" 요정이 물어요.
"아뇨, 그렇지 않아요." 나무꾼이 말해요.

〈134p-135p〉

"My ax isn't made of gold,"
says the woodcutter.
The nymph dives again.

"제 도끼는 금으로 만든 것이 아니에요."
나무꾼이 말해요.
요정은 다시 뛰어들어요.

〈136p-137p〉

And she appears with a silver ax.
"Is this yours?" asks the nymph.
"No. My ax is made of iron,"
says the woodcutter.

그리고 그녀는 은도끼를 들고 나타나요.
"이것이 당신 것인가요?" 요정이 물어요.
"아뇨, 제 도끼는 쇠로 만든 것이에요."
나무꾼이 말해요.

〈138p-139p〉

This time, she appears with an iron ax.
"That is my ax!" shouts the woodcutter.
"Thank you, I'm so happy."

이번에는, 요정이 쇠도끼를 들고 나타나요.
"저것이 제 도끼예요!" 나무꾼이 소리쳐요.
"고맙습니다. 저는 너무 행복해요."

〈140p-141p〉

The nymph smiles.
"You are a very honest man.
 I'll give you these gold and the silver axes."
"Oh, thank you so much."
He goes back home with his three axes.

요정은 미소 지어요.
"당신은 매우 정직한 사람이군요.
 금도끼와 은도끼를 당신에게 드릴게요."
"오, 정말 감사합니다."
그는 도끼 세 자루를 가지고 집으로 돌아가요.

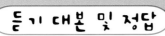
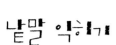

낱말 익히기

듣기 문제 ························· 146p

(듣기대본)

1. (a) bird   (b) nymph
2. (a) beautiful   (b) tall
3. (a) hold   (b) help
4. (a) woodcutter   (b) ax
5. (a) river   (b) iron
6. (a) slip   (b) fall
7. (a) this   (b) that
8. (a) silver   (b) gold
9. (a) dive   (b) three

정답

1 b	2 b	3 a
4 b	5 a	6 a
7 b	8 a	9 b

말하기 문제 ····················· 147p

1. bird   2. tall   3. smile
4. cry   5. slip   6. hold
7. three

읽기 문제 ·····················148p

1. iron   2. dive   3. cry
4. help   5. bird   6. fall
7. ax   8. beautiful   9. this

쓰기 문제 ···················· 149p

1. three   2. 빠지다   3. gold
4. 강   5. nymph   6. 미소 짓다
7. dive   8. 키가 큰   9. silver
10. 잡다   11. this   12. 아름다운
13. ax   14. 울다   15. that
16. 미끄러지다   17. iron   18. 나무꾼
19. help   20. 새

표현 익히기

듣기 문제 ························· 152p

(듣기대본)

1. (a) That is my ax.
   (b) I will wait here.
2. (a) I can help you.
   (b) Is this yours?
3. (a) Why are you crying?
   (b) My family will be hungry.

정답

1. a, b   2. b, a   3. b, a

말하기 문제 ···················· 153p

❶ Why are you crying?
❷ Will you wait a moment, please?
   I will wait here.

읽기 문제 ···················· 154p

❶ ① ❷ ② ❸ ② ❹ ①

쓰기 문제 ···················· 155p

❶ I will wait here.
❷ My family will be hungry.
❸ My ax is made of iron.
❹ I can help you.
❺ That is my ax.

Dictation

158p-159p

❶ tall ❷ birds
❸ slip ❹ fall
❺ river ❻ ax ❼ cut

160p-161p

❶ beautiful ❷ Why are you crying?
❸ woodcutter ❹ tree
❺ my family will be hungry

162p-163p

❶ I can help you ❷ I will wait here
❸ dive ❹ gold
❺ Is this yours?

164p-165p

❶ gold ❷ dive ❸ silver
❹ nymph ❺ My ax is made of iron
❻ woodcutter

166p-167p

❶ iron ❷ That is my ax. ❸ smile
❹ man ❺ give ❻ three

스토리 이해하기 ········· 168p-171p

A ❶ ① ✕ ② ○ ③ ○
  ❷ ① ○ ② ✕ ③ ✕

B ❶ ① ❷ ①

C ❶ ① help ② wait ③ woodcutter
  ❷ ① silver ② nymph ③ iron

D ❶ She hears birds singing.
  ❷ I go back home with a balloon.
  ❹ The book falls into the river.
  ❺ I give her a pencil.

183

이솝우화

부족카드

 son

 market

 donkey

 meet

 ride

 old

 talk

 father

 women

 wash

시장

market

아들

son

만나다

meet

당나귀

donkey

늙은

old

타다

ride

아버지

father

이야기하다

talk

씻다

wash

여자들

women

 clothes

 town

 boy

 carry

 tie

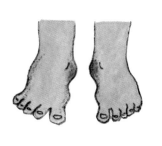 feet

 pole

 break

 catch

 find

읍

town

옷

clothes

운반하다

carry

소년

boy

발

feet

묶다

tie

부서지다

break

막대기

pole

찾다

find

잡다

catch

summer

grass

green

hot

ant

collect

sweat

under

grasshopper

sing

잔디
grass

여름
summer

더운
hot

녹색
green

모으다
collect

개미
ant

~아래에
under

땀흘리다
sweat

노래하다
sing

베짱이
grasshopper

shade

family

winter

autumn

crop

cold

shake

visit

give

close

가족
family

그늘
shade

가을
autumn

겨울
winter

추운
cold

농작물
crop

방문하다
visit

떨다
shake

닫다
close

주다
give

woodcutter

fall

tall

river

ax

cry

bird

beautiful

slip

nymph

빠지다

fall

나무꾼

woodcutter

강

river

키가 큰

tall

울다

cry

도끼

ax

아름다운

beautiful

새

bird

요정

nymph

미끄러지다

slip

help

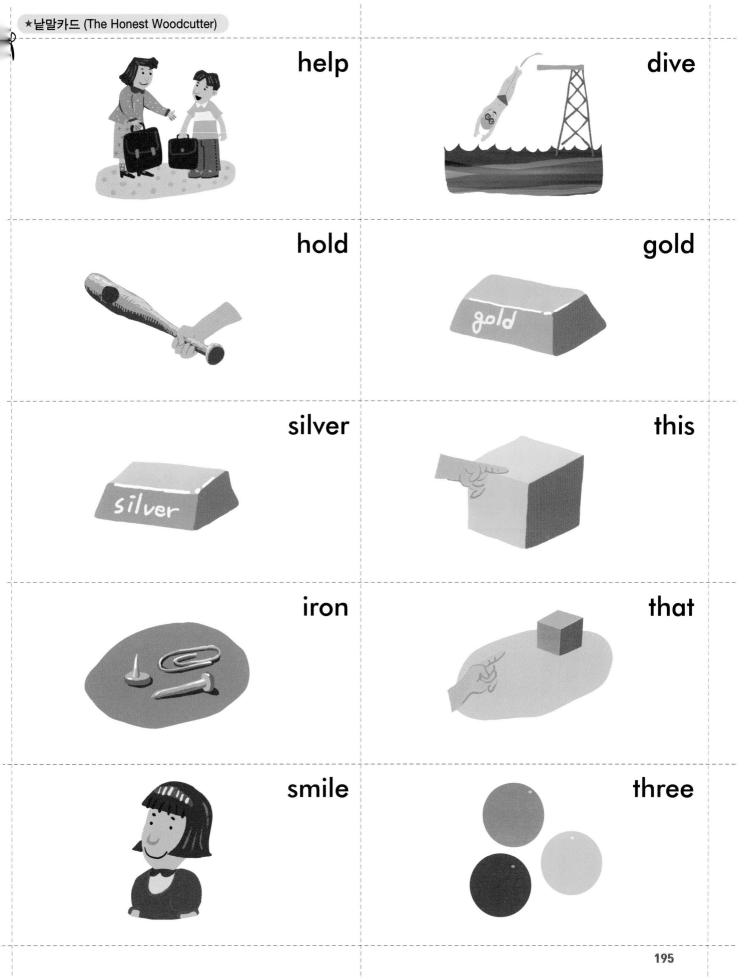

dive

hold

gold

silver

this

iron

that

smile

three

뛰어들다	돕다
dive	**help**

금	잡다
gold	**hold**

이것	은
this	**silver**

저것	쇠
that	**iron**

셋의	미소 짓다
three	**smile**

Look at that!

How stupid!

He is right.

You ride and I will walk.

Have you no respect?

Get down!

Shame on you.

Don't be cruel to the donkey!

Why don't you sing with me?

We are busy.

We must collect food.

There is lots of food.

얼마나 어리석어!

저기 좀 봐.

넌 타거라 난 걷겠다.

그가 옳아.

내려와.

넌 존경심도 없니?

당나귀를 학대하지 마세요.

부끄러운 줄 아세요.

우리는 바빠.

나와 함께 노래 부르지 않을래?

음식은 많이 있어.

우리는 음식을 모아야 해.

It is summer now.

Please let me in.

I'm very cold.

Give me some food, please.

Why are you crying?

My family will be hungry.

I can help you.

Will you wait a moment, please?

I will wait here.

Is this yours?

My ax is made of iron.

That is my ax.

나를 안으로 들어가게 해 줘.

저에게 음식 좀 주세요.

나의 가족은 굶게 될 거야.

잠시만 기다려 줄래?

이거 네 거니?

저것이 내 도끼야.

지금은 여름이야.

난 매우 추워.

넌 왜 울고 있니?

난 널 도와줄 수 있어.

난 여기서 기다릴 거야.

내 도끼는 쇠로 만든 것이야.